Poems From The Heart

The next few pages that you'll read
Were written with inspire
With the help of one person that filled my soul
With nothing but desire

The words just flowed out you see
Without any effort at all
Words to share with the world
Like writings on the wall

All these words were sparked by a woman
That I hope to never part
Enjoy my writings as you read
My poems from the heart...

ISBN-10: 0615570038
EAN-13: 9780615570037

Acknowledgments

A round of applause goes to Bryan Sevilla of Blank Slate Studios for his incredible illustration work and attention to detail.

http://www.guru.com/emp/FreelancerWebsite. aspx?id=1097958

Contents

Inside my head

♥ ♥ ♥

How can she live in my head

We have not kissed or shared a bed

Our skin has not touched

Yet I am warm inside

Just like she's here sitting by my side

I cannot wait for our lips to meet

I think that will tell us if we are meant to be

Even if we are not a match

I am happy she brought that feeling back

Inside she brought back that smile

The one that has been missing for a while

A match or not this was all worthwhile.......

The First Meet

♥ ♥ ♥

She burns inside me

It feels so warm

What I feel cannot be wrong

The first meet is behind us

It went well

Not much intimacy

She was nervous as hell

But that's ok

The bond was there,

Which will take us further

Then one could stare

I want to be with her

She knows I do

I feel her wanting

The same thing too

When I get her

In my arms again

I will hold and kiss her

But not like a friend

More like long lost lovers

That bonded again

Taking Care of You

♥ ♥ ♥

You are a giver from the start

You do it naturally from your heart

Can I take care of you?

From breakfast to dinner

You are far from a sinner

Can I take care of you?

You nurture those who are close

You never brag or boast

Can I take care of you?

In sickness or in health

You always make my heart melt

I will take care of you!

The feeling Returns

♥ ♥ ♥

I have not had this feeling for so long

Then all of a sudden she came along

She fit right into my arms

Can this do me harm?

It's like holding another heart

But can I be so smart?

To hold her gentle and not break

Her heart by mistake

Because it will break mine too

From feeling the way I do

I even hate to say good night

I rather hold her tight

I my arms where she should be

Can she be happy with me?

We will see.

Gentle Kiss

♥ ♥ ♥

A gentle kiss in the night

As you sleep tucked in tight

On your face is a happy smile

You have been sleeping for a while

A gentle kiss I place on your chest

That touches your heart as you rest

A kiss on your heart to extract your love

Is my pray tonight to God above...

You Give Me Strength

♥ ♥ ♥

Sometimes I sit and I think where I'm at

Am I in a dream or a nightmare?

Can I tell this from that?

It's a struggle at times to get through the day

So I look for a message from you to come my way

Just a simple "I miss you" can keep me a float

Any words in a note, a note that you wrote

You give me the strength to get through the day

How can I ever let you go, no fucking way!

Your Guardian Angel

♥ ♥ ♥

As you lay there down to sleep

I pray to God you're mine to keep

I lay next to you and hold you tight

To keep you safe so you can sleep the night

When you wake you will see

Your guardian angel is just me

A protector for you is my part

To love and cherish your beautiful heart

God has answered my endless prayer

Because when I awake you are there

He truly knows and can see

It's next to you I should be

Dream a Dream

♥ ♥ ♥

As you close your eyes and fall sleep

I sit here thinking of what you see

Do you dream of you being with me

Or are you counting lamb or sweet little sheep

I wonder if I'm in your dream

Or is it a nightmare of others that make you scream

To live in your heart and your mind

Is where you are in mine all the time

When I close my eyes it's you I see

Because it's with you I want to be

You are the girl of my dreams

Asleep or awake its only you it seems

Sleep tight my love and dream of me

Dream a dream of being forever with me

Knowing Me

♥ ♥ ♥

At times I don't see

What's in front of me

I assume things wrong

And argue too strong

It is ok to ask questions

But not kick up the dust

The heart has to love fully

And surrender to trust

All I want is happiness

Between you and me

To share love and laughter

The way it should be

The hurt we encounter

We should not cause

Yet to be there for each other

Not look for each other's flaws

I love you dearly

I will prove it you'll see

My heart is in your hands

And that's where I want it to be

Please wash the feeling of doubt

Out of your heart

Fill it with love

As we need a fresh start

I can go on

And you know I can too

Because I can't shut my mouth

So pinch my nipples when I see you

Night Time Reading

♥ ♥ ♥

If you wake up in the night

You will see I took the time to write

A little poem for you to see

About how much you mean to me

You are my strength you help me cope

You make rough times seem like there's hope

You are so very special to me

Asleep or awake you're all I see

There is nothing at night that I rather do

Than to lay in bed holding you

As I grow tired I just want to say

I love you more each and every day

Sleep Through the night

♥ ♥ ♥

Sleep is not what I can do

Unless I send something to you

Something for you to see

When you wake and think of me

Do you think I am crazy for doing this

Or does it make you want to kiss

Kiss me when you see such words

Is it corny to act like young lovebirds

If I don't send you something at night

I can't sleep, it just don't feel right

Every word does come from my heart

A heart full of love but aches when apart

All I want is to hold you tight

Give you a kiss and sleep with you through the night

Sleep at night

♥ ♥ ♥

As I lay down tonight

I wish I was holding you so tight

I hold my pillow close you see

Wishing it was you here with me

Every night I think and pray

That someday it will be that way.

A prayer for you

♥ ♥ ♥

Time has come for me to sleep

I thank thy Lord for her to keep

Watch this night over she

Teach her Lord to trust in me

She had a very very hard day

Give her strength and send Your blessing her way

So as I go to bed this night

I thank You again for bringing her into my life

Please bless her Lord as she sleeps

Because I gave her my heart to keep

Show me to another day

Direct my love all her way

Amen

Wake up in the night

♥ ♥ ♥

If you wake up in the night

I thought I take the time to write

A poem that you like so much

One that reaches to your heart to touch

It don't take much for me to do

Because of the love I have for you

Words flow from my heart you see

All of what you mean to me

You're the one that makes me whole

You touch my heart and my soul

The love of my life is you that I found

Now close your eyes and let my love sleep you sound

Being Apart

♥ ♥ ♥

As we part and drive away

We head on home a different way

It's is definitely not easy to just leave

My heart gets swollen and pains with grieve

I sit at home all alone

Thinking when will we pass this milestone

It gets so much harder every day

To not be with you and be away

Soon we need to make this right

For you to be in my arms every night

With all my heart I hope it comes true

Because I am madly in love with you!

Easter Prayer

♥ ♥ ♥

Oh Lord,

My heart is the first thing that she stole

Now she has been able to steal my soul

This time I am going to do it right!

I will never let her out of my sight

Lord I cherish her as a gift from You

Guide me please in all I do

I want to thank You Lord on Your holiest day

Please make sure she knows I love her in a big way

I miss her so while she is over there

Lord, blessing her heart is my Easter Prayer

Amen

Don't Want to Lose You

♥ ♥ ♥

I truly am in love with you, but I am really scared

Cause I don't want to lose you, what we have is very rare

We both are going through things, we have to

make a mend

But can we get to the next level or will I lose you in

the end?

My heart bleeds without you, I miss you when apart

The thumping that you hear so loud is the beating

of my heart

My love is unconditional I never thought it could

be true

To love you is just effortless, without you I'd be blue

If I ever lost you, I never would regret

All the great times we spent together ever since we met

I am still afraid to lose you, the fear is in my heart

If it ever comes to that day it would tear me right apart

I know you think I'm crazy but see it from my view

There is not a man on earth that wouldn't fall

in love with you

Time Goes By

♥ ♥ ♥

Another night and time goes by

Faster than a blink of an eye

Always when I am with you

It doesn't matter what we do

It goes so slow when we are apart

But when together we're so quick to depart

It gets harder every single day

To be so damn far away

I feel like an empty soul

But when I am with you I feel like I'm whole

Do you think time will go by fast

When we are together finally at last

I hope then time stands still

Because we will enjoy it, I know we will

Just know you are already missed

And as soon as I see you, you will be kissed.

Just missing you

♥ ♥ ♥

OK, so I feel a mush

All I can think about is your sexy little tush

I'm in love, what can I say

I can say, I will love you every day

Yes, it's another poem you got

It's because I love you a lot

Oh, here comes that pain

Yes when we are apart its always the same

No much that I can do

But keep on loving you and hope you love me too

Give her strength

♥ ♥ ♥

Lord, yes it's me again

Another call to You for my friend

My friend that holds my heart

You know the one I hate when we're apart

She just does not seem right

She needs more sleep at night

She is running herself down

She helps everyone while smiling, she never does it

with a frown

Please grant her strength before she gets ill

Cause she will keep going, she has a strong will

She is one of Your best!

Not to say anything bad about the rest

But this woman is my love

That's why I am praying to You Lord up above.

Pain be Gone

♥ ♥ ♥

Hurt in the eyes isn't good to see

Not for you and not for me

Especially when the love is strong

Hurting each other is just so wrong

At times it is not something we mean to cause

It can stop your heart and put it on pause

That's what happens when you feel you're all in

Being hurt by a love one is never a win

To put it behind us shows there's hope there

Just reach into your heart if there's love to declare

Be gone with the pain let it fade away

Get closer to me, don't run, just stay

Writing this to you brings a tear to my eye

It just chokes me up and I fight not to cry

Not because I am very sad

It's just because I am definitely scared

Now I know that you are scared too

But it cannot, no way stop...from me loving you

Miss You

♥ ♥ ♥

A day without you

Is like being without air

Is doesn't matter

If I know that you are there

I need you by me

To get through the day

I miss you too much

To have it any other way

My love is so strong

Yet I could feel so weak

My heart is all yours

It's yours for you to keep

The time has to come

When we're together every day

I love you so much I don't want it any other way

To have your lips

Against mine to kiss

That's all I could think of

When it is you that I miss

A Perfect Day

♥ ♥ ♥

A perfect day

Just went away

I wanted nothing more

Than for her to stay

As we drive down the highway

And we are about to part

We flash our lights repeatedly

It just breaks my heart

It's a sign of good bye

Until we see each other again

When will the next day be

When will we have time to spend

It's getting too hard to deal with

When she is away

I need her by my side daily

In such a bad way

When we don't have to leave each other

It will be the perfect day!

Every day I pray for that to be today!

Quick from the Heart

♥ ♥ ♥

I never felt this way before

To love someone each day more and more

When i am with you it seems so right

I want to be with you night after night

Gazing into your beautiful eyes is what i need

You have planted love in my heart like a blooming seed

My love for you does nothing but grow

I want the entire world to know

Just shout out "i love you" for the everyone to hear

As i hold you close and whisper it in your ear

Together we are the perfect match

How can anyone think you are not the best catch

I wrote this fast from finish to start

It came so easy just quick from my heart

I will end this poem with a simple i love you

And hope it's me you will always love too.

Don't Let our love go

♥ ♥ ♥

I love you so much

I hope that is enough

I would do anything for you

Take a bullet if that's what I have to do

There's no way I want to go away

All I want to do is stay

Stay with you forever

Though I am not the best boyfriend ever

But I promise I will try to be

So you can love and be proud of me

I hope you want to be with me each day

Because I feel exactly that way

You are the girl of my dreams

But I fucked up with you it seems

Please love me so

And don't let our love go

I have so much to give

It is you that make me want to live.

I never want to part

I love you with all my heart

Don't know what to do

♥ ♥ ♥

As I sit here on a call

There is nothing I could do at all

But think of how much I love you

And hope that you love me too

My heart is in my throat

Not hearing it as you spoke

Nor would you write

That you love me since last night

I don't want to ask you

It is just not the same

If your love is lost for me

It would be a crying shame

I don't know what to do

Because I am head over heels for you

I cannot leave you be

It is just not me

I believe is being there

Not sit aside I know it's rare

We have a special love

Sent from God above

Please don't let it go

It is killing me real slow

Carmela I truly love you

But all I feel is blue

I hope God gives me a sign

Cause I don't know what to do...

Eyes

♥ ♥ ♥

I look into her eyes

And it is no surprise

That I see the woman I love

It took many years

To find someone dear

She had to come from God above

Her eyes make see

Where I want to be

Which is right next to her all the time

It hurts to be away

It drags out the day

It feels like it should be a crime

When I hold her close

I just want to boast

On how much I love her so

I would scream it out loud

And I will be proud

I'm not shy to let my love show

When I look into her eyes

I get hypnotized

From the love that they radiate out

I want to capture that image

It's just like beautiful vintage

Because that is what love is about

An Afternoon Thought

♥ ♥ ♥

How can I think?

With her on my mind

She is a beautiful woman

Just one of a kind

I sit here at work

Missing her so

Being without her

I have nowhere to go

I sit in deep thought

At times I'm a wreck

As I miss her so much

Wishing I was biting her neck

Caressing her body

As I dig in my teeth

Bending her over

And sliding in deep

Grasping her hair

And pulling it tight

As I tease her inside

Oh I fit in her just right

What am I to do

With this afternoon thought

Wait till I see her

This thought won't be fought

Together we will be

♥ ♥ ♥

Sitting here missing you

I think of you and me

Hoping that the time comes soon

And together we will be

Not knowing if you will want it

Once things start to change

I hope you want to be around me

And together we will be

I love you will all my heart

I think you feel the same

I can't wait when you are near me

And together we will be

It hurts when I am not with you

I don't know what to do you see

I hope the time comes faster

And together we will be.....

Love Shows

♥ ♥ ♥

I just want you to know

No matter where you go

You will have with my love to show

To show how i care

Being happy or in despair

It does not matter where

I will be there

And my love will show

It will show home much you mean

Mean to me and it will seem

That you are the woman for me

And every person will see

That I love you so.

Because it will surely show

Words for the benefit

♥ ♥ ♥

At the benefit she will walk

With some friends and they will talk

I'll sit at home and be so blue

When i am without her that's what i do

I miss her so when we're apart

It's hard not to when she owns my heart

A relay for life is a good cause

But with her there and me here I feel so lost

I hope she feels the love I send

My love for her will never end.

I need you

♥ ♥ ♥

When I am wrong I know I am

I will be sorry and change I can

We I love I love for all

There will be no one else I want to call

I need you in my life you see

I need you to be with just me

I will correct what hurts your heart

Because without I will fall apart

I need you to be with me now

Don't shut down I would want to die some how

I am in tears because I pushed you away

Don't go anywhere please please stay

I need to hold you or I will die

My heart is exploding on my oh my

Don't shut down its killing me

I can't back off and let you be

I love you with all my heart

If I don't see you now I will just fall apart

final Prayer

♥ ♥ ♥

Now I lay me down to sleep

Lord please make this be the last I weep

I close my eyes and I hope to see

You my Lord just take me please

It hurts so much to deal with stress

Take me Lord as I rest

Have my soul rise in the air

Let this be my final prayer

Lonely at The Inn

♥ ♥ ♥

All day long we were together

Nothing more could be much better

Yet the loneliness sets in

When she leave me at the inn

She heads on home in the night

It feels so wrong, it's just not right

In my arms she should be asleep

Instead she leaves my heart to weep

At this point it's not her fault

Though it causes my heart to halt

Call me selfish not wanting her to part

But I'm not greedy when it comes to the heart

I give her my heart and my soul

Sometimes separation takes its toll

Know it is not just about me

It's about us as a couple is where I wait to be

To want her as my true partner is no sin

There won't be any more loneliness at the inn

A Prayer to Bond

♥ ♥ ♥

As I lay me down to sleep

Without her here I start to weep

I pray to God to give me strength

To make it to the next time spent

Lord please make the day come real soon

When we sleep together under the moon

I need her by me in my life

I hope someday to make her my wife

I look to You to help us through

To the day we bond and say "I do".

Amen.

A Poem with Just Meaning to You

♥ ♥ ♥

Here's a poem as I am up all night

Counting the hours to hold you tight

Tears run down my face as I miss you so

Thinking that tomorrow I must go

It breaks my heart to leave you here

When I need you close and near

This next week will break my heart

With all the shit going on and being apart

I will try to stay strong but can't promise a thing

I hope when apart you will feel my heart sing

This poem just has meaning to you

I am sorry it reads nothing but me being blue

Do know I love you with all my heart

That's why these things are so hard

Feeling Blue

♥ ♥ ♥

Dealing with some days are really hard

Especially when we are far apart

It bleeds my heart when you hurt

You should be crying your tears upon my shirt

Being on the other end of the coast

Breaks my heart when you need me the most

Talking on the phone is not the same

I need to hold you and take your pain

Not work, not home, not money matters to me

You are the most important thing to my heart you see

When the day becomes really tough

Know in my heart I love you oh so much

You are the woman I hope to keep

In my arms each night when we sleep

So when you're down and feeling blue

Reach out to me because I love you....

finding a Match

♥ ♥ ♥

You spend part of your life with someone

To realize they are not the one

You hang on to the end

A lot of time you spend

And it all amounts to none

Then you meet up with another

You both click like no other

Your love grows each day

You love the new way

Always wanting to be with each other

Finding your match feels great

All the time you had to wait

If it is real

And that's what you feel

Don't stop your love or hesitate

When love is right

Its each other you like

You feel each other's heart

When together or apart

Just stay close & hold each other's heart tight

When you find your match don't let go

You will feel inside and you will know

Show your love each day

In a special way

And together your love will grow

My Stay

♥ ♥ ♥

Yes I am up late my dear

Thinking about my stay here

How fast it went being with you

Time flies by no matter what we do

It will break my heart when we part

Staying away from you just don't seem smart

I need to be with you every day

The thanks I give is for my stay

Soon I will have you in my arms

That's when I rest nice and calm

I love you I don't want my stay to end

You're my heart, my lover, and my best friend

Never Too Old

♥ ♥ ♥

When the night is in

And the day is gone

My mind races with sorrow & song

Though some thoughts are sad

And others are bright

It's my love for you

That makes it all right

We carry a torch of past pain

Our hearts need to work together

To put out that flame

When we get past it we will be free

To hold each other daily like we want it to be

Never too old to find happiness again

As you're the love of my life & my best friend

Thankful For

♥ ♥ ♥

Today I woke up to see

More than the sun shining in on me

I saw that you are a great find

A love for me, a love of mine

You came to my side when in need

You shut the world off to be with me

Things like that captures my heart

Life with you is really a fresh start

Today its "you" that I am Thankful For

That God let me find you at my front door

Past, Present, Future

♥ ♥ ♥

Bottom line, Bottom of the list

You say it's not true

Oh how I fuckin wish

So many obstacles get in the way

Deal with it Paul, if you want her to stay

Climbing the ladder to be even seen

Not top priority, time is so lean

Things to get done, just stop and wait

Other things are important, just table our fate

Change in direction easily done

Being alone with nowhere to run

Available by convenience makes me feel last

It crushes my heart ever so fast

Am I your present or do you want me to last?

Am I your future or will I be just your past?

Together we are strong in so many ways

But when we're apart your attention don't stay

My hearts in shambles it's shaking for you

I tremble from the love, what can I do

Your past & present leave but your future will stay

Will your future have you sleeping on my chest, is

that right way?

What Do You Think is Best?

♥ ♥ ♥

Can I recreate the lost poem that said a lot?

I don't know but I can give it a shot.

The poem had meaning and was to reach into your mind.

To see if it is in sync and aligned with mine.

It was not a poem like all the rest.

It was a poem that asked what do you think is best?

How do you feel about being mine?

Are you ready? Do you want it? Or it is not the right time?

You come from a relationship of over 30 years.

Are you sure you want to be committed with me here?

Committed apart is different you see.

Committed together is where I want to be.

A great girlfriend you are and I'm happy you see.

But partners in life is what I want for you and me.

Do you really want to sleep every night on my chest?

Tell me how you feel and what you think is best.

There are 2 things about you that scares me to death

But the thought of being without you takes away

my breath

I think of the holidays with family and friends

I think of you me together right to the end

You are the last person I want to see before I close

my eyes

And the first person to I see in the mornings sun

filled skies

Let me take care of you I will cherish your heart

Don't push me aside it tears me apart

You know that I love you and I think that you see

That all that I want is for you to be with me.

I assume that you know that I am not like the rest

But for you, just yourself, what do you think is best?